'Thommie Gillow's poet[ry] challenges your perceptio[ns,] feelings and strong words, [with her blend] of humour and intelligence. Highly recommended for anyone who's ever been human.'
Ruth Baxendale – Poetry Co-ordinator Manx Lit Fest

'Thommie is an innovative writer and natural performer who engages diverse audiences by presenting universal themes with unique personal twists and a dark sense of fun.'
Dr. Matthew Alford – Film critic

'Her witty, tongue in cheek, quirky poems and down to earth performance style has won her cascades of applause whenever she takes to the stage.'
Gina Sherman – Apples and Snakes

'A brilliant performer – Gillow has great stage presence and an easy rapport with her audience. Her poetry is at once moving, thought-provoking and damn funny.'
John Quirk – Manx Lit Fest organiser

Thommie Gillow spent her early years in Bath where she discovered a love of poetry, but it was not until her family relocated to the North East that Thommie grew old enough to have her heart broken by many of the men who have influenced the poetry in this book. She lived and worked in several countries before settling down to become an English lecturer back in the South West. A single mum to one daughter, Thommie has a Masters in Creative Writing from Cardiff University and has twice been shortlisted for the Bridport Poetry Prize.

THOMMIE GILLOW

MY STEPMOTHER TRIED TO KILL ME

Burning Eye

Copyright © 2014 Thommie Gillow

The author asserts the moral right under the Copyright, Designs and Patents Act 1988 to be identified as the author of this work

All rights reserved. No part of this publication may be reproduced, stored in a retrieval system, or transmitted, in any form or by any means without the prior written consent of Burning Eye Books, nor be otherwise circulated in any form of binding or cover other than that in which it is published and without a similar condition being imposed on the subsequent purchaser.

This edition published by Burning Eye Books 2014

www.burningeye.co.uk

@burningeye

Burning Eye Books
15 West Hill, Portishead, BS20 6LG

ISBN 978 1 90913 625 0

*For all my wonderful and terrible ex-boyfriends,
thanks for the inspiration,*

to Arthur and Angela for setting everything up,

*and for Susanna, Hope, Joe and Mum,
for the continuing love.*

CONTENTS

- 11 Poem About a Shoe
- 13 Neal Robbins – The Old Goat
- 18 Newspapers
- 19 Driving on the M5
- 23 Spreading the Love
- 26 Sasha
- 28 85210
- 30 Poem for Ed
- 34 Huntsman
- 35 The Present
- 38 Small Daddy
- 43 The Reason I Only Take Selective Compliments
- 44 Chemistry Lessons
- 46 Thelma
- 48 My Batman
- 50 My Perfect Man
- 52 A Poem on Request
- 54 A Good Wife
- 55 She Who Did Me Wrong
- 56 The Dress
- 58 Doing Spells with Sophie
- 59 My Rock Musician
- 60 In the Outback
- 61 Traffic Lights
- 62 Psychoanalysis
- 64 America
- 65 He's in Love with Me
- 66 This is for You
- 68 Butterfly: Mine
- 69 The Woman's Secret
- 70 Breastfeeding
- 72 The Poet and the Neurologist
- 74 The Changing of the Spots – Parenthood
- 75 Maybe
- 76 Pamela Anderson
- 77 My Stepmother Tried to Kill Me

A Poem About a Shoe

I received a letter from your solicitor
saying I really must stop writing poems about you,
                              or you will sue.
She said, *my client insists that you refrain
          from slandering his name
          in the public poetry domain.*

So here
let me make this very clear,
this is not a poem about you,
it is not a poem about
a man who screws around,
it is not a poem about boozing,
                    losing,
                         drug choosing,
smirking,
work shirking or
just general jerking   off.
This is not a poem about you,
this is a poem about a shoe.

Once upon a time across a crowded room I saw a shoe
and he came up to me and he said, *Hey you,*
and I said, *Who?* and he said, *You,*
and I said, *You talking to me shoe?*
and he said, *Yeah you, how do you do?*

We seemed to fit and for a while
there was nothing that I couldn't do with my shoe.

We were in step with each other,
walked astride with each other
our souls fused like the marbled pattern
on the rubber of your wellington boots
we seemed to suit.

We were tied together, me and my shoe.
I felt he would heel any previous woes
and he so wanted to, he caressed my toes
and let his tongue go loose.

Then one day
my shoe said   Hey
       there's something I've gotta say,
       I wanna stray.
       It's just something us shoes have gotta do,
       though it's less about me and more about you,
       seeing other feet it's like shoe porn,
       I can't help it I've got the shoe horn,
       I wanna indulge myself in fetish play
       and by the way
       your best mate wore me yesterday.

Once upon a time across a crowded room I saw a shoe,
I only wish I knew then what I know now,
that my best friend is a cow,
and that it is never a good idea to buy a sofa, with a shoe.
especially when that shoe's a loafer, like you.
so I say this to your solicitor and you.

Go ahead and sue,
              or just shoo!

Neal Robbins – The Old Goat

When I was 17, it was me
and Neal Robbins,
together
forever,
– in my head.
I just never told him so.

If you'd asked me I would have said;
I love him more than my own good health
more than riches and wealth
more than life itself
but I'd have been lying.

I wanted that romantic dream
we all want when we're 17
I wanted love that makes you bleed
transcends human greed
and makes you believe
if you're together,
that's all you need.

But me and Neal? We'd never succeed.

When I was 17 it was me, and Neal Robbins
together, forever
or so I willed it,
until the day I killed it

We were walking in the woods,
I rather imagined I was a fairy,
light and airy
dancing in the shafts of sunlight through the trees.
I thought I was ethereal and free.

I had never felt more beautiful,
I'd planned my clothes and boots

and made my hair curl
to subtly tempt,
I knew he liked the outdoor girl,
and this look?
It was rugged and unkempt.

I danced along the path,
enjoyed his gaze,
wished only to amaze
with my carefree spirit and laugh,
to show him I was the one.
I danced and spun
and twisted and twirled
and exclaimed beautiful extravagant statements
like, *It's such a glorious world,*
and, *isn't it all so wondrous!*

and I knew
that this was finally the time
Neal Robbins would see
                            me
and become mine.

I was 17,
the lure of the river was too much,
How could he resist a girl who walks on water?
I would be Persephone,
Zeus's daughter,
freed from the underworld
for my precious time with him.

He watched my grace,
this was our day,
finally
our place.

So I tiptoed stone to stone,
the sparkles in the river
were sparkling in my hair.
There was no-one else but us there,
and I didn't want to miss
the perfect moment to kiss
the start of our lifelong affair,
so when I saw it I knew it was a gift from nature,
that perfect stone.
Large and grey, rounded and smooth,
this was the place to make my first move.

I'd step lightly onto it,
spin and he would sweep up behind
arms around my waist
press his lips down on mine so I could taste him.
It would forever be a beacon to love
that stone,
that perfect mottled grey stone
and we would embrace
he'd look softly into my face
and say,
Now Thommie,
now I see
it is you and me,
together
forever,
for eternity
we're meant to be.

I glanced behind,
he was watching, waiting,
so with my heart beating and quickening pulsating
I reached the stone,
like a podium calling this:

> *come come, come come my dears and kiss*
> *come come, come come my dears and kiss*
> *come come*
> *come come*
> *come come my dears and kiss.*

I put out a foot,
swung my hips forward,
with grace began to transfer my weight
but wait,
as my foot was descending
and my gravity shifted
I saw that this stone had legs, head and throat,
too late,
my leg was too far gone to be lifted
as it broke the ribs of this rotten dead goat.

The crack echoed through the trees.

With a whoosh like an explosion
the internal decay and corrosion
rushed putrid gas up my nose,
yellow pus streamed from it
and I began to vomit
and felt decomposing flesh round my toes.

The river was no longer sparkling
but full of swirling clouds and mist,
the perfect stone was no longer a stone
and gone was our perfect first kiss.

He took me home in his Mum's jeep,
with cellophane on the seat
and plastic bags on my feet,
but we never did kiss,
he never held me close,
look into my eyes
and realise
the future I wanted the most.

And now, though I am no longer 17,
no longer obsessed with teenage dreams,
and happy in my life without him,
Neal Robbins,

I still feel like there's a little sick on my chest,
every time he rejects my facebook friend request.

When I was 17 it was me,
and Neal Robbins
together
forever,
or so I hoped,
until the day we went for a walk
and I trod on a dead goat.

Newspapers

You read me as if I am a newspaper.
You flick through my pages to the parts
that interest you, the cartoons,
page three, you ignore the rest.
You don't read my article on *Men who
don't recycle*, and my career advice
makes you turn the page.
You like the letters, other people's
comments matter to you.
You don't much care for my
response or where my bias lies.
You never think about the hands
that have written me.

Soon you will discard me as if I am
done: a newspaper you have read.
You will neatly collect my
supplements together and throw me
in the bin with your potato peel
and empty bean cans.
You will forget that I had breath.
You will forget that there were pages you
didn't understand.

Then one day, when kindly hands
have recycled me you will look down
and find that my ink
                        has stained you.

Driving on the M5

When I was driving to see you in your hospital bed
and the traffic was tailing back on the M5
all I could see was a neon light flashing in my head
flicker flicker flicker   red
cruel and harsh against the night,
that word
Meningitis.

We didn't see you enough I kept telling myself,
a few hours up the country and we let months pass sometimes,
like climbing in a car and losing a few hours was impossible,
or just not practical
or all in all too difficult when we live our lives.
And I was suddenly filled with hatred for your wife
– whom I love –
because she got to be with you everyday
and as your sister I lived 100 miles away.

I was lost in my own private disco of car lights
with indicators and brakes and orange street lamps
and beeping as the night traffic trundled on.
There was screaming in my head
and a rudimentary understanding of that word,
Meningitis, the word that put you in the bed,
and the other word, the one no-one said.
What happens? What happens if the worse happens
and if when you get there he's already…?

When we were children you made me sick you were so loving.
It was like you'd taken a sweetness pill overload
and learnt to write the word love before any other.
To my wonderful amazing sister,
I love you love you love you, you wrote,
for years.

Every birthday card you handmade I kept
so I could laugh at you and ridicule it,

your extremities of love.
But on that journey
on that night,

flicker flicker flicker   red,

I realised that the cool child I thought I was,
was the one who'd have regrets
I was the one who hadn't said
I love you love you love you enough.

When I was 12 Dad fought with me
because my room was messy,
and the clash of our egos did the rest,
We screamed and cried and threw words
only me and Dad threw
because Mum and you,
you were too gentle.
First minute you're back, he yelled,
you tidy that room like your life depends on it,
and he gave me that look so I knew
that was what I would have to do.
But 3 hours later when I came home
and was frog-marched upstairs,
with threats of
you'll stay there all year if you have to
'til I can see that carpet again
and
no daughter of mine is going to live in a pig sty.
and
you'll get all sorts of diseases.

I opened the door
and the room was tidy.
Clear floor, made bed
and books all neatly lined up on the shelves.

How the hell...
and I turned my head to see you winking:
My yucky, mucky, stinking brother,
you've always looked after me like no other.

Flicker flicker flicker   red
that word in my head.

I don't know if there was a moon that night,
but I was grateful for the road works and the bollards
forcing me to drive slowly.
Around me people in cars
picked their noses
and sang along to the radio,
they didn't know,
there wasn't a neon light in their heads,
and the best person they knew wasn't in a hospital bed.
You knew how many chevrons there are
on that stretch of road,
you used to count them so you could win silly bets.
Northbound eighty-seven I think,
       an odd number.

In amongst a sea of people I'd never felt more alone,
so I promised this:
I promised God, the ether, mother nature, the earth,
I promised anything that would listen,
give me my brother back,
make my brother well
and I will never do wrong again,
I will phone him every day and
never take him for granted.
Say it's all a misunderstanding
and I'll be a better person,
I won't drink

and I promise I'll never think
bad thoughts again.
Give me my brother back,
I will always appreciate and love him and
never ridicule him for his soppiness or bad hair.
Give me my brother back
and I swear
I'll take in any homeless person you send to me,
do any good that you set for me
but please,
God, ether, mother nature, earth
anything that's listening please

flickering flickering flickering   red

when I get there,
let my brother not be dead.

Spreading the Love

I'd like to tell you a story
about a woman that I know
at heart she is a poet
but she sidelines as a ho.

Yes she's a prostitute,
she's a real good-looker,
she's a woman of the night,
she's a real classy hooker.
She's a real go-er
and she says it's not a crime,
but all the time she's doing it
she's doing it in rhyme.

She met a man one day,
who thought that she was cute.
She said he'd have to pay,
he said, *I've got a lot of loot,*
have you protection?
She said, *I've condoms in my boot,*
which just in case you're wondering
is right down on my foot.

Yes she's a safety queen,
she'll tie you on the bed
but use a dental dam
if you wanna give her head.
She won't catch 'owt from you
but she'll show you a good time
and all the time she's doing it
she's doing it in rhyme.

He had a lovely night
and a lovely morning too
as he lay there contemplating
that last night's poetic screw,

and he set about his day
with a post-coital glow
                on show
                until
he tried to speak
and he tried and he tried
and he began to weep
and he cried and he cried
for the words were still coming
but not quite as you'd know it.
His nookie, with Cookie,
had turned him to a poet.
His sentences were rhythmic,
his meter quite refined,
and all the time he was saying it
he was saying it in rhyme.

Some time passed
and I decided to befriend her.
What happened there? I asked
She said, *I have my own agenda,*
I will keep it clean
but I do just what I can
to spread a love of poetry
throughout the modern man.

Oh yes a condom's great
for stopping HIV
and use a Durex, Mate
for no unwanted pregnancy.
Sticking socks on your cocks
stops STIs of sorts
like chlamydia and herpes
and crabs and genital warts,
but there's one secret something
that I'm spreading all the time,
it's what I gave to him
it's the STI of rhyme.

So if your pals start talking in stanzas,
your mates start talking in verse,
your next-door neighbour uses haikus,
or limericks or worse,
if your uncle starts barking orders
with little rhymes at the end,
you know,
and I know,
that they have known
my friend.

Sasha

If I eat three Weight Watchers Mars bars
does that count as a binge session?
and when David comes home from
not quite working and complains because
I hung his saggy elastic boxer-shorts up
outside the flat where our only neighbour
could see them but the air could make them
smell so fresh do I ask him about the
cauliflower and garlic he forgot to buy?
Do I moan that I am the fabric of this sari
we are woven up in and yet I have lost
my beginnings, and my end? Should I?

I open the fridge and see that the C.I.A.
bugged my parmesan due to the fact
it has been so long sitting there it is not at risk
of escape. I knew there was a buzzing
on my phone line but thought it was the flies
around the nappies David refuses to touch.
He says the korma stains deter him and he
has such sensitive skin. The baby doesn't
cry anymore, not since prohibition and
that man who masturbates in our cellar.
I pinched him the other day to check
that he was real and he laughed.

David likes to watch the television and calls
the remote Suzie, like a girlfriend
he had in school. She let him shag her places I have
never let him near and I don't mean Bracknell.
I spend my evening finding alternative places
to hang the baby grows and wonder if
my ears might be a good solution, and my
coat-hanger nipples. I used to jingle if
you shook me out and my gold threads catch the light,
yet now my step hardly breaks the flow
of the Daily Show, or the slapping from the basement.

If I eat three Weight Watchers Mars bars
does that make me a binge eater? Does it make
me real? If I eat three Weight Watchers
Mars bars will it help me breathe?

85210 – France

He stands outside his door like a sentry,
guarding, watching as the English family
drink too much in their holiday house next door.

His mother, Bernadette, will die next year,
of old age, and poor nutrition. She will
leave him a fifty-four year old orphan
finally with a room to call his own.
At first he will be sad when his body
creeps over to her side of the bed
but that will pass.

                    The English family
laugh at him, Gérard, in his beret.
He unnerves them, always watching, guarding.
Even his French is old-fashioned and rough.
Gruff, gruff, gruff, he says nodding his head
to the men. The girls he merely stares at.

Next year, when Madame Bernadette is gone
the English will giggle. *He will surely die
they say, he is clearly an imbecile.
Without his mother barking orders
how will he know to buy the bread, or milk,
that come from the lady in the white van.*
In fact, when she does die, he will just drink
and continue staring.   *Pauvre Gérard.*

The English family buy his home-made wine,
'pineau', 'eau de vie', from the cellar.
Bernadette tells him it's poison, like that
which killed Papa. He *bofs* in response. *Bof.*

The middle of nowhere, 85210 – France,
Gérard watches as an English family
frolic and drink cheap wine. They run about
in scanty bikinis and laugh at him:
the sentry next-door neighbour guarding them.
He does the only job he's ever known
from thirty years national service past.
The boys stick two fingers up and smile,
knowing he will copy them, think it's a game.
He laughs when they laugh, continues staring.

Madame Bernadette inside, in the bed
she shares with her son, continues to die.

Poem for Ed

I want to get myself a religion,
I want to find me a God who will help me
through these hard times
and give me a greater reason for being.
I want to feel insignificant, and small,
like my pain is all just part of the plan for us all.

I want to experiment with Buddhism,
reach enlightenment and stop this fire
that scorches through me
every time I think of you.
I want to meditate and forget everything,
I want to wear orange, or blue
and cross my legs
in oh so many ways.
I want to transcend.
I want to be past caring about the things you say
and wondering why it is that
you will not be my friend.

I want to come back
as a domestic cat,
I want to sleep all day and occasionally catch a mouse for fun and
be fed gourmet food by an over-indulgent owner who strokes me.
I want my owner to be a stoner
and I can sit really close and get passively wasted
but at the end of the day I'll be a CAT,
so you can't blame me for that.

I want to be wicca
I want magic spells to get me through the day,
I want to burn candles at both ends and will you back to me,
inscribe your name
in wax and
gaze at the flame
and say it again,

Bring back my love
though I did not deserve him
bring back my love and I will not lose again.

I want to be Jewish
I like circumcision, it works for me.

I want to be pagan.
I want to ask the spirits of
the north, south, east and west
to help me rest,
to bless
me,
ask the earth
to stop quaking beneath my feet,
and the air
to stop being so heavily scented of you it
cakes my lungs and holds you in me,
I want to ask the water
to stop swilling out my womb in all that hollow space
from our child,
the one I never had.
I want to ask the fire
to stop burning me,
to stop flaring in my veins
     at your name
to stop raging in my core
like my pain is its coal and its wood and its paraffin,
and God I'm a bore,
this is why I've started looking for
a religion.

I want to be mormon,
I could be one of your wives,
we could share.

I want to know Islam
I want to put my life into the hands of the prophets,
live my life as I'm told,
and not with this free will that so destroys me.
I want to stop drinking and purify my soul,
I want to do it for Allah,
I want to know that if I can't have you
I can still have happiness as a goal.
I want to know
I am doing my best for my immortality,
because maybe in the future we could be,
or in the next life, you'd be there waiting for me.

I want to be one with the earth,
I want to have peace,
I want to have someone greater than me
who can forgive me,
or guide me,
or make me feel that everything happens for a reason
and whatever doesn't kill me WILL make me stronger,
and that that is why it happens,
because
I must be strong.

I want to stop believing in Karma, the bitch, I hate her,
I want to stop yelling at her and asking her why? why?
when all I've ever done is try
to be a good person,
and yes I know I stole once from a charity box when I was nine
but I didn't take it all, and I collected it anyway,
and I know I told a lie when I was seventeen, a bad lie,
but why karma? Why does it always rain on me?

And I want to stop quoting Travis lyrics
and thinking they were right.

I want to replace karma with Quakerism,
I want to be quiet,
for a long long time.
and pause
and breathe,
and stop all this crazy talking.

I want to get me a religion,
I want to find a way out of thinking of you.

Huntsman

Steve tells me his business deals in gemstones,
he illegally crosses the Thai/Burmese
border on foot and goes directly to
the miners. He tells me this is ethical
because the miners make more money without
the government taxes and customs on
the export. He snorts a line of cocaine
and eyes up a redhead sitting opposite.

Steve hasn't brought his Thai girlfriend Malee
with him to the UK and dismisses
her with a sneer when I ask. *She's pretty,*
he says, *but there's no shortage of young girls
looking for a westerner in Thailand.*
The redhead downs three shots and throws her head
back. Steve watches. Her left boob slips out
of her dress but she doesn't see, just drinks.

Steve offers me a sapphire, he says he hates
the stone but has respect for those who love it.
He says he could have spotted me anywhere,
a sapphirophile. I look at my fingers
and my wrists. *The mark up does not benefit
the miners,* he says, *but I have resources
they don't, that they could never hope to access.*
I watch the redhead sway on her seat, smear her
lipstick with the back of her hand and hiccough.

Steve is watching too, absentmindedly
flicking his fingers on his pint. I want to ask
how many have died for a stone he hates but
I don't want to know his answer. He tells me
pure ethics are impossible in South East
Asia and that he does not feel compromised.
The redhead is sick on the floor, hanging over
her table like a master-less dance puppet.
Steve stands and goes to her, *I'll take you home,* he says.

The Present

I'm going to give you my body
You're gonna smile and say thanks
and treat it with the awe it deserves.
You're gonna celebrate my curves,
and feel honoured that you've had to wait
all these years
for this gift that I now can see
is the greatest part of me.

I'm going to give you my hands,
for too long they've obsessed
with washing up and holding pens,
I'm going to put my hands
      in your hands
      and they'll be friends
our fingers will interlink
and the dirty dishes will stay in the sink
and your hands will teach my hands new things.
They'll caress my palms.
I'm going to give you my arms,
and my shoulders and my elbows
I'm going to give you my toes.
Even the big one with the toe nail that fell off
because I did too much running
and you can take them to market
or let them eat roast beef
who knows?

And the mole on my back which I've never seen
but that I know isn't malignant thanks to modern medicine
I'm going to give that to you too
because sharing is what my body and I like to do.

I'm going to give you my tummy
etched as it is with the lines I'm a mummy.
There's a map of the London underground on my midriff

and this is my gift
my body with its markings of life
and who cares if I can't go on trampolines anymore!

I'm going to give you my creases and my bumps
and my lovely lady lumps,
and my saggy bum
and the cellulite on my thighs
and my eyes
which cry too easily
with joy, with pain, with love, with despair,
eyes that look and see
(albeit with glasses now)
eyes that care
and you know what?
I'm going to give you my pubic hair
because it's glorious
and it grows everywhere.

It is not perfect this gift,
it is not airbrushed or photo-shopped or moulded,
there are places it used to be young and fresh
but has now been corroded,
it's been overloaded,
but it stays standing, it rises,
and these saggy breasts that once seemed like compromises
are just badges of honour that it succeeded
when milk was needed.

It hasn't been artificially sucked or tucked
and let's be honest this body has probably been fucked
too much
it drinks alcohol
and it sweats
but never forget this body is living,
this body is giving,
this body is magnificent, splendid, superb,
if life were a language this body's a verb,
it's a doer, a goer,
a clarinet blower,
and it's not by chance
that this body can dance.

I'm going to give you my body
and you're going to smile and say thanks
and tell me no better body exists for you anywhere
and that you love it,
that you'll never share
and you'll run your fingers through my hair and
thank my feet and legs and hips
and torso and shoulders and neck
for keeping me standing there.

I'm going to give you my body.
It's the most amazing thing
that's got me everywhere.
I'm going to give you my body,
treat it with care.

Small Daddy

Oh Small daddy,   oh daddy Small,
I have seen you walking in your night gown,
and flip flops.
Knocking on windows
shouting through locks
you, who never sleeps,
you, who never weeps.
Oh Small daddy,   oh daddy Small,
the blood we once shared is now mine for keeps.

You send me £30
I give you an R
you phone to tell me you are struggling for cash
and you know I cannot sleep with you daddy
Small   oh Small daddy
I say I'll send the money back
but that's not what you mean, you say,
you mean, you say,
you mean, I mean.
You mean, mean, mean.
I give you an E.

Which world taught you about money
Small daddy?   daddy Small?
the YMCA?
Or the banks in Croatia, Belgrade?
Parenting made easy by Natwest
or HSBC
by ATMs
and money transfers.
Oh Small daddy,   oh daddy Small,
I have seen the cheques you use
to fill hearts
to teach
to motivate, inspire,
I have seen you reach
into your pocket

and pull out only receipts
on fire.
You give me a pair of purple gloves for Christmas
nothing more, nothing less
and I give you an S,
Small daddy,   oh daddy Small.

Your father was a better man
Small daddy,   Grandaddy,
daddy grand,   grand daddy.
When he came to see the child
he brought smiles,
and eased himself down stairs
with no banister.

When you came I hoped you
would offer love or counsel,
but no Small daddy,   daddy Small
you proved
when the apple leaves the tree
it falls very far indeed.
Small daddy,   oh daddy Small
she is only a baby
my baby,
my rock-a-bye lullababy,
you ask me, *how much?*
I give you a P.

And this short term history repeats
repeats
repeats.
You Small daddy were never a role model
and they cry, the women at your feet.
There is a baby here, and a cheque,
one there, one there, one there,
and how many more down drains
or in cardboard bedpans?

Daddy daddy daddy daddy Small,
                      oh daddy Small
to be faithful is unnatural
to be fair
       be fair
              be fair.
History repeats
             repeats
                    repeats.

Let your penis rise high above the people
Small daddy,   daddy Small,
the people of Welwyn Garden City,
let it grow
before the people of Riga, of Reykjavik
let ordinary women drown in your semen
then say 'Abort, abort'
for there is only so far money can go.
Grandaddy, daddy Small rolls
       over
              and over
                        and over
I give you an O.

Oh Small daddy,   oh daddy Small
you have no excuses,
there is always a bad Kate waiting in a bar
always a mother alone with a babe
there is always a set of ridiculous parents
throwing money at psychiatrists
that you don't need
and paying your rent.
Oh Small daddy,   daddy Small
your money is spent
and you forgot to buy self-worth or respect.
The baby is mine
when she cries

I rise,
no matter when,
Small daddy,　　　　　　　daddy Small while you roam
the streets
for your conquests
she feeds from my breasts.
I give you an N.

For every bad Kate there is a good Kate
who finds the only thing of beauty left in hell
and hands it to me.
I keep it, she is mine, yes mine yes.
I give you an S.
Yes Small daddy,　　　　　　daddy Small
there is such a thing as child support,
abort, abort, abort
would hold more weight had you not tried
for this child.
I give you an I.

I give you a B
– for baby, remember that word?
daddy daddy daddy　　　　　　　　Small.
I give you I.

The L is an easy gift, I wish it on you every day
I wish you L
I give you L
Small daddy,　　　　　　　daddy Small,
you both.
Take it.
Take it.
Take it.

Take it daddy
take it daddy
take it Small daddy,　　　　　daddy Small.

It offers salvation.

Take it and turn your plane tickets to mulsh
to pulp
take I and T, take IT
stop your fancy cameras and expensive dates,
stop your affairs, your selves,
stop your lies.
take Y
stop asking questions
stop asking questions
stop asking questions
stop.

The answer is easy Small daddy,   daddy Small.
The answer is easy.
The baby is mine.

The Reason I Only Take Selective Compliments

He never thought I was beautiful,
he said as much, trying to buoy me up with
my FANTASTIC personality. He never
let me wear short skirts or make up
or be like the other girls. In fact one night,
he sent me to a night club in his dinner jacket.

He said, *You light up the room*
and, *Don't worry, there's someone for
everyone,* and, *I think my hairdresser
fancies me, she asked what I'm doing tonight.*

After one particular row that lasted for years
he said, *I thought that you were ugly
when you wouldn't speak to me. Your
letters were so cruel, ugly actions, ugly girl.*

He told me everything was okay because
my mother wasn't all that hot either
and hadn't she done well for herself with him.
She used to be a model. He bought me Doctor Martins
because I didn't have the legs for heels.

I diet before I visit him now, and always say
no to ice-cream, he says it contributed to the divorce.

I'd like to believe you when you say
I'm beautiful and say, *Thank you,* as I know I should,
but I'd rather you just tell me I'm nice
and that I have a FANTASTIC
personality.

Chemistry Lessons

She agreed to date him
because she was bored.
And lonely. And because
she hadn't yet learnt about
chemistry. She kissed him
because that is what she
knew, and blithely
took his virginity like it
was a leaflet handed out
on the streets. When he got
down on one knee she
smiled and enjoyed the
attention, agreed, of
course, and played the game.

Then one day she looked at him
and saw that he was handsome.
He took her to his Mama's
and she saw that he was doting.
He wanted her children
and she saw that he loved her.

So she stopped.

He was Italian, he did what
Italian men do.
He sent her a four-leaf clover.
He told her she was still
      the air he breathed.
He wrote her songs and
sang in husky basso profondo.

She moved on.

Ten years on and she has learnt
about chemistry – the hard way,
                      with the explosions.

She has learnt to clear the debris.
She thinks he still remembers her,
she still remembers him.

Thelma

Thelma, who lives in a damp high-rise flat,
wonders if her bi-polar son will ever
come home for Christmas. She cries when the voices
tell her to bolt her door. They say she has
a beautiful mind, they say she should have
accepted the offer made by the little
Christian girl who delivers the papers.
Next year she will, God willing.

                                    Thelma worries
about the size nine boot prints left on the wall
of her grey entrance hall, and hides behind
the sofa, with a cushion on her head.

The little Christian girl has a mother
who comes to visit in the middle of
the night and brings with her a priest. Thelma
undoes the chains and safety locks: the voices
say she must trust in God. But the priest is just
the devil in disguise, and not her son.
No choir of angels sing carols around him.

The little Christian girl's mother holds Thelma's
hand, and leads her past the yobs who defecated
on the *Welcome* mat, though no-one believes it.
Two demons disguised as doctors prod her,
and together sign a paper. She remembers
Herod's treachery and yearns for her son.
The mother signs the paper too – a section.
It is not the paper her daughter delivered.

Next year, God willing, the little Christian
girl will give the old lady who lives in
the housing association flats up the road
the bubble bath she saved her pocket money
for. Next year, God willing, Thelma will hide
behind little Christian sofas and wonder
if her bi-polar son will find her, should he
read the address she left pinned to her door.

My Batman

Before I met you I was strong,
there was an iron rod down my spine
and I knocked away potential foes with the back of my hand
like a synced together version of a Jackie Chan movie
and old school batman,
hi ya, biff bam, kapow, kazam

When you came close I shot you back with a fist,
with a thump, with a push to the left,
and jolt to the right,
I whacked you hard across your chest
and said don't even think about it mister,
I can burn you, so you don't even blister,
I can throw you seven feet across the room
and not even break a nail,
don't even think about it mister, you will fail.

So you didn't
even think about it,
you didn't
even try
and you turned your back on my kickboxing antics
and let it lie.
You were always polite and when I came close you said 'hi'
but never gave me time for –ya, or kapow,
never let me biff bam you
or kazam you.

When I met you I was strong,
I had armour steeled from the hardest of pains,
you couldn't have speared me
anymore than you could have cut salami with a plastic knife,
so you didn't,
you got on with your life
and there was no opportunity for crunch and whaap,
for ouch, or zap
no time for thonk, or zlonk, or klonk,

and I might have been strong,
but here was a man
who stood proud,
and after the first rebuffal never again allowed
me to wham him, biff baff him, kazam him.
and I realised I was wrong.

When I met you I was strong,
but now after six months in your arms
the electric currents don't run through my shield anymore,
they run through my pores,
and the acid I used to spray out in my poetry
is just soppy love stuff
that makes even me want to be sick
and I wrote it!
I can still hi-ya, and kapow,
but now
I've also learnt to kiss
and that comes with a whole different kind of kazaam.
I have the world's best man,
– he taught me this:

>   If you value yourself enough,
>   real strength comes
>   from being brave enough to love.

Hiiiiiiiiiii   YA!

My Perfect Man

If I had to describe my perfect man
he wouldn't be you.
He wouldn't talk the way you do,
or walk the way you do,
and he wouldn't wear
                his hair
in that stupid style the stupid way you do.
He wouldn't be you.

My perfect man would be tall,
not small – the way you are,
and he'd be rich.
He wouldn't be poor like you,
and sure as hell
he wouldn't snore like you.

No he wouldn't be you.

He'd buy me chocolates
with the personal touch,
rose creams, my favourite,
just a hint, not too much.
My friends would adore him,
he'd help out with their issues,
and they'd all cry before him,
and he'd pass them the tissues.
He wouldn't dismiss their heartaches
as desperate harpies,
and huff down to the pub
with a grab of the car keys.
He wouldn't be you.
He wouldn't moan,
and he'd always hear the phone,
the way you never seem to.
My perfect man just wouldn't be you.

He wouldn't watch Star Trek,
he wouldn't swear,
he wouldn't wake me up in the night
with some pathetic nightmare.
He would wash his own socks,
        and put them in pairs.

He wouldn't like football.
Leave it at that.
No football.
NO FOOTBALL.
What's that?
Liverpool scored? Steven Gerrard is fit!
No NOT AT ALL.
I don't give a shit.
No FOOTBALL!

If I had to describe my perfect man
he wouldn't he wouldn't he wouldn't be you,
my perfect man just wouldn't be you,
but then he wouldn't be my perfect man
if he weren't you.

A Poem on Request

Like many men before you, you ask me for a poem,
this is the curse of my calling and my love life.
But soon I realise, as you continue your request,
that you do not wish for a poem, like the rest.

You say
don't mention my name
be discreet
be subtle
be sweet
just make a secret joke as an aside,
don't let it be known it's me that you describe.
You say
don't talk about my beard
or my long curly hair,
don't say my friends think I'm weird
but I don't even care,
and don't at any point, refer to my saggy underwear.

Just a little nod will do,
a private thought between me and you,
so only I know
and you know
what you're referring to.

You say
I'm an entomologist
employed ecologist
don't mention that,
it's too identifiable,
you say
don't write a poem about slugs or beetles or locusts
it's just not viable,
your style is far less nature focussed.

You say
don't make it clear it's me you refer to,

write a poem about opera, or poetry, or shoes,
or your daughter, not me.
Just stick in a little extra line
that's mine.
Write about your passions,
write about your life
your worries, your fears, your troubles and strife,
write from your heart
not some forced loving trite.

So I say,
alright.
And like many men before you I write the poem you asked me for,
and this one is not shite,
it goes like this;

M is for mummy, as I always will be,
I is for the importance of that to me,
K is for Kate and Vicky my friends
and E is for where this poem ends,

Put them together if you so like,
but there's no relevance to the fact it spells Mike.

A Good Wife

I wanted to let you know that I did your washing,
I hung it on the radiators and
put the heating on so it would dry.
I even ironed it.
I am a good wife.

I thought I should tell you that I made your dinner,
I tried to get the balance between carb and protein
the way you like it.
I laid it out on the table with a napkin and a steak knife,
and washed the pans.
I am a good wife.

I'm just touching base, but by the way
I wanted to say
that I am sorry for the times I had a headache,
I didn't mean to, it just happened,
and sometimes alcohol can prompt these things,
one way or the other,
as I know
you also know.

And I wanted to tell you that I've thought about
the weight I put on whilst pregnant and you are right,
I should have taken better care.
You needed a wife
who'd love you
and one you could be proud of.
And I see now how unreasonable my expecting you
to be up in the night with the baby was.

So I just wanted to let you know that I did your washing
and that I'm sorry of course,
but today dearest husband,
I filed for divorce.

She Who Did Me Wrong

She's as ugly as a bulldog,
without their bright eyes,
and it really wouldn't matter
if she was nice,
        but she's not.
She's a slob.

She's as manipulative as a politician,
without the charm,
and it really wouldn't matter
if she didn't do such harm,
        but for now,
She's a cow.

She's as vindictive and jealous, as selfish and cruel
as a fox crossed with a vulture,
a crocodile with a witch.
She's a bitch, bitch, bitch
but it really wouldn't matter one bit,
if he hadn't fallen for it.

The Dress

There is a place,
not a hundred miles from here
where clothes moths lay their eggs
like rice droppings on the carpets
and apples sit pickling in un-operable drawers.
That is the place
you'll find her.

She hangs
wrapped in black nonwoven PP
watching the dust patterns swirl in the cracks of light.
Crammed in with a disused golf caddy
and stale air.
Hidden from prying eyes,
from ever-eager ebayers who know no values,
and the moths feast on her broken promises.

For it is true, I once hoped for more.
I hoped for stains on cushions
and freshly baked buns.
I once believed in purity, in white, in diamonds,
but now the only white there encases a larvae
that eats her flesh in order to live,
that and the white of mould
when even pickled apples grow too old.
I used to see her diamonds sparkle.

There is a place
not a hundred miles from here
where dreams that were woven into fairytales
hang,
awaiting execution.
That is the place
you'll find her.

Send her my love,
remind her of those times as children
when we played together.
Tell her I've grown up now
and just one lie?
Tell her I grew wise.

Doing Spells with Sophie

The cat burnt her whiskers last night,
we'd been doing spells and left the candles burning.
Cindered cinnamon scattered around
cauldrons churning,
                    bubbling, frothing wishes.
And the cat burnt her whiskers.

An omen perhaps?
A lapse in our concentration,
our hell bent determination,
our magic weaving, cult believing, meditation,
until the yelp, the *owh*,
the *help*, the miaow.
The cat burnt her whiskers last night,
it gave her a fright.
but was a funny sight.

My Rock Musician

Archetypal sixth form fuck up
                            ten years on,
but still sexy.

Out

      of

his

      mind

still.

You know the kind?
                Still sexy.

Deep
incomplete
boozer, loser, drug chooser, screwer
archetypically screwing, screwing, screwing
                                    screwed

up!

But still sexy,

      ten years on.

Oh fuck!

In the Outback

Mile upon mile of red sand, stretching onwards before me.
Flies buzzing, tickling, bugging,
hours of heat,
      monotonous conversations with myself.
Dead kangaroos,   and vultures hovering,
      assessing my health and general well being.
      Such thoughtful creatures.

Skies so clear and so close and so blue,
      the dark matt tinged with an orange purple hue.
And the sun beating down,
      beating now,
waging war against us all,   and winning.

On I walk,
head down,
kicking the stones as I go.
Thumbing a lift from a random man in a pick-up truck,
      and who gives a fuck?

Mile upon mile of red sand
and a dream I once held in my hand.

Traffic Lights

It's night.
The traffic lights turn red,
>   painting the pavement I walk upon
with disco lights,
and orange,
>   and green,
>   >   and go, go, go.
Like a dream.

There's dancing fairies in the colours
and the rain.
Sparkling like little stars,
secret remarks whispering go, go, go.
And the colours, and the lights.
Orange,
and red.
>   Stop.
>   Dead.
Like a dream in my head.
>   Just as you said.

It's night.
The town buzzes as the pubs close,
gently vibrating with the noise
>   and the squalor.
Cars and crowds, and cars in crowds and crowds in cars.
>   (and dancing fairies, like little stars.)
No fights,
just traffic lights.
Red, like a past,
orange, like a memory,
and green,
>   go, go, go.
Like a dream.

Psychoanalysis

I used to possess the phallus,
> but I'm giving it back to those dominant patriarchs
> who denied me it in the first place.

For years you told me I missed for it,
> I longed for it,
>> begged for it,

and cried for the child I was before castration.
For years you told me of my missing strength
and I learnt to fight my sexist nation.
Until I won,
and my penis came home.

But this phallus restricts me,
conforms me to a world of male supremacy.
Makes me an honorary man,
> a wannabe man.

The phallus made me think I was strong,
> I was wrong.

So have it back dominant ideology,
have back what you said you took from me.
Stick your dick, your knob, your cock,
I never liked it all that lot.
I had more all along if only I'd known,
that I don't need your phallus with a mind of my own.

So thank you Freud for my castration.
Thank you Adam for my rib.
Thank you Cixous for my liberation
and thank you patriarchs for my dick!

But really thanks for wasting your time,
I was conned for a while but I've opened my eyes
and I'm really much happier with my own mind.

I used to possess the phallus you see,
but it never looked that good on me.

America

I bought a vibrator today,
I'm in America,
       that's what they do here.
Bold as brass, that's actually shaking inside,
I held my head high,
walked into the shop and smiled.

For I am English,
       and my upper lip is indeed stiff,
       – no pun intended.
My normal purchases so far from such feminist liberation,
this American influence would do well to infiltrate my
guilt-ridden nation.

So there I was,
lost in a selection of longs and shorts,
       wides and narrows,
              wiggly, jiggly, giggly, rubber latex, waterproof toys.
Who needs boys?!
Not I, I say.
I'm in America.

He's in Love with Me

He's in love with me,
he just doesn't know it yet,
and it's not that I don't love him,
but ignorance kills,
it's the price we pay.

One day he'll know,
when we're older and I'm far away,
and he'll say to his beautiful wife;
there was this girl I used to know,
Jennie,
she was different, special.
I was in love with her,
though I never knew it.

And wherever I am,
in my place far away,
I'll smile.

Because he's in love with me,
he just doesn't know it yet,
and it's not that I don't love him,
but ignorance kills,
it's the price we pay.

This is for You

This is for you,
you sad, pathetic, mind blowing drug.
To think I let you fuck me up.

The first time injected,
such fluid in my veins
that desire I detected
and lived to bear the blame.
That desire turned to hunger
and hunger into need,
a thousand die there desolate when hungers choose to feed.

And that limp flesh in my hand,
alive without a breath.
A spliff I smoked again, again,
addicted,
       'til the death.
Or lesser fate,
but time was moving on
       and open caverns closed their liquid gates
            too late.

Held the drug against my skin
with love: its sad disguise.
Those the lows that became my life,
the drug? – my search for highs.
As if a male narcotic disguise
       would give us better lives.

A drugged disease of rotten sort,
an evil skank,
a cruel skunk,
so I forget,
       I ever drank,
       or played.

Was ever young,
        or innocent.

I've been through cold turkey now,
I'm done with oblique misery
and that drug addicted soul you knew
no longer lives with me.

For you,
you poisoned opium,
a drug addicted life I led
and such constricted blood I bled.
But I'm through now,
I'm done.

I've had cold turkey,
I've lost the taste of bitter sperm,
                of you.
This is for you,
      you venomous lust,
      you atheist angel dust.
You sad, pathetic, mind blowing drug.
To think I let you fuck me up.

Butterfly: Mine

I saw her pretty coloured dress
and tender wings that flew.
She danced and twirled and twisted and spun
as she floated down the blue.

The men in the big flying bird
had dropped her off for me.
They set thousands of fairies free then,
but she danced for only me.

I let her find her resting place,
and ran over the dusty floor.
I bent to pick her up my fairy,
I don't have an arm anymore.

The Woman's Secret

I have not a size six waist and skinny chest,
can't wear high heels and short skirts like the rest.
Don't slap concealor or make-up on my face
and with friends of my years I feel out of place.
I can't slip into dresses made for girls of my age,
at the click of a finger have a teenage rage.
My lips aren't rouged, fluorescent red,
and hairspray and gel aren't found on my head.
But yet in my walk there's a womanly way
that's attractive to men and the games that they play.
It's a swing of the hips, a click of the heel,
that outweighs the giggles for female appeal.
And my friends they say to be like me they yearn,
for I have something, they're yet to learn.
I have the secret that all women hold,
the young, the middle-aged, and still the old.
And I look at the girls, each made-up face,
each shiny shoe and tiny waist,
and know that someday they'll know what to do
so that they might have the woman's secret too.
                    Do you have it?   I do!

Breastfeeding

It's the middle of the night
all is calm
outside a street light glows orange
illuminating the people carriers
and Volvos.

Suddenly I wake
pulled from my dreams
vanishing memories of my pre-pregnancy body
yanked out with her screams.
The charm breaks
and my breasts burst
I am awash with milky glue.
She carries on screaming
angry with thirst.

They ache
these mammouth Jordan-esque melons
that throb and pulse and stretch to fill
and though the rivers run into puddles on my pillow
the oceans rage in my mammory glands still.

So I rise
to her cries
and sulkily stomp to her room.
How can he sleep through?

And as I knock my head on her mobile
and my grandfather's clock chimes three
I reach over the cot to my daughter
she stops her screams
sees me
and smiles.

And through all the sleepless nights
the body cavities and pain
with that smile all is forgiven
      – until she wakes me up again.

The Poet and the Neurologist
(first published in the Journal of Neurochemistry 2013 vol 127)

When the poet met up with the neurologist
the first thing she said was this,
how is it?
that my brain,
with all the wonderful things it is,
has not yet learnt to kiss?

How is it that I cannot open my head,
and take the thread
of my thoughts
and tie them to yours,
intertwine us together,
make you mine again, forever?

To me your words taste like wishes,
dropped deep into a well
clinking like fishes
echoing
bellowing
yellowing in the canals of my mind.
To me your neck smells of promises and fear,
and if I could open my skull to you
you would see electricity through my glia,
bolts and lightening strikes on fire
through my glia,
and each word that passes your lips
you'd see my dopamine levels get higher and higher and higher
and then you'd see them dip.

If my brain could hold yours it would hold yours
in hands as big as arm chairs,
as big as hippos
for all that it thinks it knows
only with your brain could mine ever really smell a rose.

Rip open my skull
and my brain will wave at you,
it will spill down my spine in its longing for you
reaching out efferent fibres, limbic desire.
Crawl through memories that crown us,
through memories that drown us,
through memories we side step lest they indelibly stamp us.
Rip open my skull
and you will see my hippocampus
flushed with you.

It has been too long neurologist
and my poetry has turned my brain from matter into smoke.
You once said my love was a joke,
a bio-chemical reaction
so each time we had sex
I tried to open my cortex to you
so you could see each hemisphere glow
and know
that my love was true,
but it was more than I could do.

When the poet met up with the neurologist
the first thing she said was this,
how is it? I ask you why,
that my brain,
with all the wonderful things it is,
it has not yet learnt to kiss
goodbye?

The Changing of the Spots - Parenthood

Your spots have changed my dear,
said the leopard to his wife,
I have been watching you lie there in the shade
and seen them cluster like ink blots.

There are patches now that are
missing, places I loved to run
my tongue across your fur and feel
the unknown of the black beneath.

There are parts that were once
beautifully smooth yet now are patterned
I see what was white has become black
and black to white. In only a few

hours you have become another
cat. I would not recognise you
from the pack. Your spots have
changed and you are holding yourself

in a different way, as if your spots
have bolstered and yet softened you.
I have been watching you lie there in the shade
and before my eyes you have gone all Rorschach.

Your spots have changed my dear,
said the leopard to his wife.

Yes, she replied, I know.

Maybe...

Maybe I'm mad
or a little crazy
or I had a bump on my head that I didn't even register
that washed away my blues
and clouded up my view
with you.

Maybe I'm wearing rose tinted glasses as corneas
and my real glasses are just a veneer
of respectability.

Maybe I should never have started this poem
because I hate Valentines, it's all tacky and commercial
and I just spent £2.99 on rubbish you'll probably throw away
or maybe that's just what I say to seem cool.

But you?
You are cool
and you're mine
and I think about you all the time
like a scratch on a CD
you and me
you you you you you and me
and I know it's crazy
and that maybe it's not enough
to just tell you I'm in love
and that I don't understand how the rest of the world
isn't wrestling me for you
but for now
that's all I can do
that
and thank you
for moving in
and loving me too.

Now get your arse in gear,
I want to be married this year.

Pamela Anderson

Pamela Anderson looks like me,
or at least she thinks she does.
She's got what makes men go, *Wow!*
And me too, they love us.

They don't have cardboard cut outs of me,
or kiss posters of me on their wall,
but where ever I go they're sure to follow,
for I am like Pammie, after all.

Her blond hair makes tongues fall out,
my red is covered in gel,
but she modelled herself on me you see,
they sucked her and tucked her quite well.

For I have lovely thoughts you know
and if nice thoughts make beauty,
I look like Pamela Anderson
and she modelled herself on me.

My Stepmother Tried to Kill Me

My stepmother tried to kill me
in the wind and the rain and the snow.
She tried to kill me in the sun
through the ribs of my back, past my heart.
She tried to kill me when the mist settled
choking, choking me on truths that she couldn't get past.
She replaced me twice,
with stick creatures in different languages
a strange concoction of dialect twangs
and foreign colloquialisms.
And then
just when I thought she was done,
she replaced me again
with another one.
My stepmother tried to kill me
with words.

My stepmother tried to kill me,
damn near succeeded one morning,
after that night I silently beat her.
When I punched her away from my father,
I left no mark, no witnesses, no proof.
With the testimony of a liar
my stepmother tried to kill me.

Mirrors broke in our hallway,
heavy mirrors,
hung so long on the walls
the paper behind had different stains.
Shafts of glass glittered on the carpet
sending back splintered reflections.
There comes a point in every life
when even mirrors who cannot lie
cannot continue to view the world upside down.

My stepmother tried to kill me
in the wind and the rain and the snow.
She married for love – you know:
love makes you do funny things.
Every day she polishes the floorboards,
and the silverware
and the apple
shines so brightly you could see your own likeness.
She bought me red shoes to dance in,
but gave them instead to her stick babies.

My father made his bed on broken mirrors,
and my stepmother tried to kill me.